BEDE AND THE PSALTER

BENEDICTA WARD

SLG Press
Convent of the Incarnation
Fairacres Oxford OX4 1TB

ISBN 0 7283 0159 8
ISSN 0307-1405

Bede and the Psalter was originally given as The Jarrow Lecture at St Paul's Church, Jarrow, 1991 and is reprinted with permission.

ACKNOWLEDGEMENT

The cover illustration is from *The Book of Beasts*, by T.H. White, Jonathan Cape, 1954, and is reproduced by kind permission of David Higham Associates Ltd.

Printed and Bound by Will Print, Oxford, England

Lord, what love have I unto Thy law; all the day long is my study in it.

(Ps. 119.97)

DURING Bede's last illness his constant companion, the monk Cuthbert, noted that after giving daily lessons to his pupils Bede would spend 'the rest of the day chanting the psalter as best he could'[1]. Other saints have also died with the psalms as the basis of their prayer: Augustine, for instance, in the fourth century, had the seven Penitential Psalms always before him, and Teresa of Avila in the sixteenth century repeated over and over again the verse from psalm 51, 'a broken and a contrite heart, O God, thou wilt not despise'. The hundred and fifty psalms of the Old Testament have always had a central place in the tradition of Christian prayer, but it is not immediately clear why that collection of Jewish prayers and poems should be words for Christians to live and die by. The Jewish psalter was naturally the prayer book of Jesus and the apostles, but it became the prayer of the early church in spite of, rather than because of, its Jewish roots. The psalms were composed by David, who was the ancestor of Christ, and each was therefore seen as a particular prophecy of Christ. Paul recommended the Christians in Ephesus and Colosse to celebrate their redemption 'in psalms and hymns and spiritual songs' (Eph. 5:9; Col. 3:6) because already they were redolent for them with the good news of Christ, but these reasons for love of the psalms are not the most vital. The basic reason why it is the psalms that strengthen dying men is surely that the evangelists, in recording how Christ on the Cross used the words of psalm 22, 'My God, my God, why hast thou forsaken me', and for his ultimate prayer, psalm 30, 'Father, into thy hands I commend my spirit' (Luke 23:34 and 46) adduced the highest possible instance of their use.

The psalms have been used by Christians in three principal ways and Bede was concerned with each of them. First of all, there is the public, corporate recitation of the psalms, as praise and adoration, as repentance, intercession and petition, which the church, the body of Christ, offers to the Father, that sacrifice of praise to which Benson of Cowley gave the title 'The War Songs of the Prince of Peace'. Secondly, there is the scholarly, academic approach to the psalter which is concerned with the words themselves. And thirdly: personal meditation on the psalms in the long tradition of *compunctio cordis*, that bright sorrow without which Christianity is merely a religion and a rite. The use of the psalms in the liturgy shaped Bede's mind throughout his life more consistently than any other text and in both scholarship and in prayer he made major contributions to their use.

The Psalter and the Liturgy

The psalms were used in public corporate worship from the earliest times,[2] those psalms which were appropriate being selected for prayer at the beginning and ending of the day. John Chrysostom, Bishop of Constantinople and the focal point of the liturgical life of its church in the fourth century, recommended the psalms for all times and occasions in a lively sermon, with the refrain: 'first, last and central is David':

> If we keep vigil in the church, David comes first, last and central. If early in the morning we chant songs and hymns, first, last and central is David again. If we are occupied with the funeral solemnities of those who have fallen asleep, David is first, last and central.

Not only in the solemn liturgies of the great church, he says, but in all gatherings of Christians, learned or otherwise, the psalter is central:

O amazing wonder! Many who have made little progress in literature know the psalter by heart. Nor is it only in cities and churches that David is famous, in the village market, in the desert, in uninhabitable land or if girls sit at home and spin, he excites the praises of God.

Clearly, he is talking about all the holy people of God in their ordinary ways of life, not the specialist category of monks, for he then goes on to mention them:

> In the monasteries, among those holy choirs of angelic armies, David is first, last and central. In convents of virgins, where are the communities of those who imitate Mary, in deserts where there are men crucified to the world, who live their life in heaven with God, David is first, last and central. All other men at night are asleep, David alone is active, and gathering the saints of God into seraphic bands, he turns earth into heaven and converts men into angels.[3]

For the whole church, the psalms were uniquely prized and, like all Scripture, they were seen as more than human words, for in them God spoke through David as a prophet of Christ. In various ways the liturgy indicated to believers that the Jewish psalms were illuminated by the light of Christ falling upon their pages. The liturgical year itself gave new meaning to the same psalm as it was selected on different occasions: for instance, the verse from psalm 24, 'Lift up your heads, O ye gates, and be ye lift up ye everlasting doors, for the King of Glory shall come in', takes on a new meaning whether it is sung at Christmas, to signify the entry of the Lord into the world; at Easter, to signify his descent into hell; or at Ascension, to signify his entry into the gates of heaven. The addition of other words could also interpret a psalm, the simplest being the conclusion of each psalm with the words: 'Glory be to the Father, and to the Son, and to the Holy Spirit', directing the prayer to the Trinity. Antiphons— phrases sung either before or during the chanting of the psalm—served to bring out the Christological significance of the psalm. Collects also interpreted the words of each psalm; these were prayers read at the conclusion of a psalm or group of psalms to direct prayer towards Christ.[4] A text which combines the liturgical use of psalm 24 with both antiphons and prayers is the one which Bede sang in his last illness:

> O King of Glory, Lord of Might, who didst this day ascend in triumph above all the heavens, leave us not comfortless, but send to us the Spirit of the Father, even the Spirit of Truth. Alleluia.[5]

From the beginning of his life at Wearmouth, Bede heard the psalms sung by his brothers, and he set himself the task of learning them by heart. When he joined Ceolfrith at the newly founded monastery of St Paul at Jarrow, he found that Ceolfrith had established there 'the same complete method of chanting and reading which was maintained in the older monastery', although not all the twenty-two members were able to chant or read in church. Four years later, Bede, competent in both chanting and reading, had vivid experience of the importance of the tradition of the Christological interpretation of the psalter, if, as I think most probable, Bede is to be identified as the boy who survived the plague of 686 with Ceolfrith:

> In the monastery over which Ceolfrith presided, all those brethren who could read or preach or recite the antiphons and responds were taken away, with the exception of the abbot and one little lad who had been reared and taught by him, and who is at this time still in the same monastery where he holds the rank of priest and both by written and spoken words justly commends his teacher's praiseworthy acts to all who desire to know of them. Now he (I mean the abbot) being much distressed by reason of the aforesaid pestilence, gave command that, their former use being suspended, they should go through the whole psalter, except at matins and vespers, without the recitation of the

antiphons. And when this practice had been followed not without many tears and lamentation on his part for the space of one week, being unable to endure it any longer he resolved once again that the customary order of the psalms with their antiphons should be restored.[6]

'Tears' and 'lamentation' indicate considerable distress, and I do not suppose that Ceolfrith was so upset at having to omit the antiphons simply because the Offices sounded more impressive when sung in full, nor out of a legalistic sense that everything must be said. It was, after all, perfectly acceptable to simplify the Office in this way, and such a practice was recommended in the Rule of St Benedict. The words of this account convey a sense of intolerable loss which surely must have come from the absence of the antiphons whose words made the psalms into Christian prayers. Ceolfrith's devotion to the psalter was outstanding even for his own times: at Jarrow he recited the psalter twice daily in addition to the Offices, and on his last journey to Rome he 'daily chanted the psalter of David in order three times over'.[7] For him as a Christian, the psalms were the basic scaffolding for all his prayer. His influence on Bede was profound in this matter of the psalms, no less than in scriptural commentary and in doctrine.

The story of Ceolfrith and the boy Bede indicates that the psalms were used with antiphons at Jarrow in Bede's time. There is no direct information about the Office at Wearmouth-Jarrow before or during Bede's life. There are, however, certain influences that can be conjectured: the first is the Office as prescribed for other monastic houses, perhaps especially that outlined in the Rule of St Benedict. It is tempting to cut the Gordian knot and assume that Benedict Biscop and Ceolfrith used the complex arrangement of the psalms for the Office according to the Rule of St Benedict, but there is little evidence, apart from the respect shown by Bede for certain chapters of the Rule,[8] that it was any more than one rule among many which the abbots drew upon to organise life in the new monasteries. Moreover, the arrangement of psalmody in the Rule of St Benedict was something left specifically to the discretion of the abbot.[9] Ceolfrith was well acquainted with the custom at Ripon where, according to Eddius Stephanus, Wilfrid had introduced the Rule of St Benedict, which required monks to be instructed in how to 'make use of a double choir singing in harmony, with reciprocal responses and antiphons'.[10] But Ceolfrith had begun his monastic experience in the Irish monastery of Gilling, and also knew the monastery of Botolf in Suffolk and another monastery in Kent, while Benedict Biscop knew the Offices at the monastery of Lérins, and at St Peter's Canterbury as well as at the various monasteries and churches of Rome. Just how distinct the Offices in these places were from the Office in the Rule of St Benedict at that period is not clear, but it seems safe to assume that the whole psalter was recited each week, the major part of it at the Office of Vigils during the night.

The Offices at Wearmouth, whatever they had been like at the monastery's foundation, were further shaped by the, customs of seventh-century Rome. In 679 Benedict Biscop and Ceolfrith had visited Rome together, and there Pope Agatho had agreed to allow John, the precentor of St Peter's and abbot of the monastery of St Martin, to 'teach the monks of [their] monastery the mode of chanting throughout the year as it was practised at St Peter's in Rome'.[11] The cantors of the monastery therefore learned the distribution of the psalms; the order and manner of singing and reading aloud; the lessons and texts of the antiphons and responds; and the cycle of feasts in use at St Peter's.[12] They learned not so much from books as from a performer, and among the children of the monastery who heard him at that time was Bede, who entered the monastery in 680, the same year that John came to Wearmouth. By the time he went to Jarrow, he knew the psalter and was well able, unlike some others, to practise this new method of chant. The basilica of St Peter was the focus of the devotion of pilgrims and especially of the Anglo-Saxons, and the founders of Wearmouth-Jarrow could find no better model for their own devotions.

The Office at St Peter's, which John brought to the north, had been established in the second half of the seventh century. It was above all an audible Office, based on scripture. This Roman tradition of chanting the psalms so that they could be heard and understood spread widely, and later could be insisted upon as the true norm. At the Council of Cloveshoe, for instance, one chapter insisted that the psalter should not be sung 'to the tragic tone of the poets' but straightforwardly 'according to the Roman use', while another explained in detail the obligation upon monks and clergy to base their worship directly upon the psalter.[13] In Bede's homilies there are references to this custom of chanting psalms and scriptural canticles through the night at vigils, especially at Easter and other great feasts where the psalms were interspersed with scripture readings. In a sermon for the dedication of a church he writes:

> We traditionally spend the night vigil joyfully singing additional psalms and hearing a large number of lessons, in a church where many lights are burning and the walls are adorned more lavishly than usual.[14]

Canticles—other sections of biblical material arranged for singing—were also included in the rest of the Office; for instance it is clear from one of Bede's homilies on the Virgin Mary that the Magnificat was sung at Vespers:

> It has become an excellent and salutary custom in the church for everyone to sing this hymn (the Magnificat) daily in the Office of evening prayer.[15]

Bede also commented on the canticle of Habakkuk,[16] another text used in the Office, and here his interpretation of the words was also predominantly Christological.

How were these psalms and canticles sung? Presumably, with the single voice of a trained cantor for the psalms, with the repetitive sentences of antiphons as a chorus, either at the beginning and end or repeated after each or several verses. Aethelwulf, describing the chanting a century later in a cell of the monastery of Lindisfarne, says of Siwine, the fifth abbot, that

> when the reverend festivals of God's saints came round and when between two choirs in the church he sang the verses of the psalms among the brothers, they rendered in song the sweet sounding music of the flowing antiphon; and the lector, a man very learned in books, poured forth song to the general delight, singing in a clear voice.[17]

Psalmody was not a new tradition in Bede's day in England; when Augustine came to Kent, he and his companions met in the church of St Martin to 'chant the psalms' first, and then to 'pray, to say mass, to preach and to baptise';[18] Aidan and his companions 'occupied themselves either with reading the scriptures or learning the psalms'.[19] It is no wonder that Bede, their historian and heir, placed the psalms at the heart of his life in 'the daily task (cura) of singing in the church'.[20]

Bede as a Scholar and the Psalms

Bede had, then, a thorough knowledge of the psalms, and in their Christological aspect they formed the structure of his thought. The psalter was central for him in solitary prayer as well as in the daily Offices because it spoke about Christ For him it was natural to learn the psalter by heart, one psalm learned and repeated after another: in this he and Ceolfrith were typical rather than exceptional. Wilfrid also had learned the whole psalter by heart at Lindisfarne, in the old version of Jerome; he was able to change the entire mental structure of his prayer when he was in Rome by learning by heart a second psalter, that of Jerome's *iuxta hebraicos*.[21] It says much for his powerful intellect that he could do so. Bede also used the same two psalters, presumably both known by heart. As a child he was taught the Gallican psalter, Jerome's first revision of the Latin psalter and the one used in church, and it was this that he quoted in his writings and which he also used in his *De Metris et Tropis*. On two occasions, however, he used Jerome's later version, made from the Hebrew—once for scholarly purposes and once for prayer. One manuscript of the psalter of very great, indeed unique, importance was transcribed during Bede's lifetime in his monastery at Jarrow. This is the *Codex Amiatinus,* the oldest extant copy of Jerome's complete Vulgate Bible, which has for its version of the psalms the third revision of Jerome, *iuxta hebraicos*.[22] The three great pandects made at Jarrow under Ceolfrith may well have owed their text to Bede's scholarly eye; certainly his care for Jerome's text *iuxta hebraicos* was in line with the text of the psalter produced for that book. The author of the *Life of Ceolfrith* refers to one of these Bibles as 'the pandect which I mentioned derived from its Hebrew and Greek originals by the translations of Jerome the priest'.[23]

The form of the Jarrow Bible belongs to the tradition of the *Codex Grandior* of Cassiodorus, but it was 'the new translation' that formed the text.[24] Ceolfrith added these 'three new copies of the new translation of the Bible' to his library. Perhaps it was Bede the scholar, who most of all delighted in this new text 'according to the Hebrew' especially for the psalter, who suggested this change. These books were not after all meant for use when singing in church but for consultation at other times:

> He (Ceolfrith) caused three Pandects to be transcribed, two of which he placed in his two monasteries in their churches in order that all who wished to read any chapter of either Testament might readily find what they desired.[25]

Whether or not Bede had seen a Bible connected with the name of Cassiodorus,[26] he knew very well his commentary on the psalms. He had other commentaries to hand, certainly those of Jerome and Augustine, and as a scholar 'following in the footsteps of the Fathers' he used them to further his understanding of the psalms. Their brilliant analysis of the words of the psalms in which they explored every shade of meaning, grammatical as well as spiritual, did as much to colour Bede's understanding of each verse as did the liturgy. Bede never claimed to have made a commentary on the psalter himself and in the *tituli psalmorum* which is attributed to him, it is Cassiodorus who is his main source.[27]

There was another text in which Bede the scholar explored the psalms; this was *De Metris et Tropis*[28] in which Bede, who called learning and prayer 'my delight', made the psalms a delight in another way also. For Bede the psalms were prayer and prophecy, but they were also poetry, and poetry as great or greater than any of the classical pagan poets. In *De Metris et Tropis,* Bede used verses from the psalms to illustrate his conviction that they contained examples of all the classical metres of poetry and in a finer way than in any secular verse. There was no need, he said, for the English Christians to pluck the rose of doctrine from among the thorns of the pagan poetry; the psalms of David, the sweet singer of Israel, offered examples as great.[29]

Bede and the Tradition of compunctio cordis *in the Psalms*

Knowledge of the psalms was integral to Bede's daily work as a monk, and as a scholar he subjected the text of the psalms to constant exploration; but there is a third way in which Bede both used the psalms and influenced their use. This arose specifically out of the context of his life as a monk, and out of the interior aspect of prayer known in the monastic tradition as 'compunction'.

In the desert of Egypt, among the first Christian monks in that explosion of ascetic life in the fourth century, the psalter was used as the basis of prayer in a special way. Here, two things are evident: first, the psalter was learned aurally by men for the most part unable to read and without books; it was learned by heart and therefore the obvious way to memorise it was to recite one psalm after another. And secondly, because the monks were not performing a ritual which changed with every liturgical season as in a church, but were following a life of prayer in their cells, the interiorisation of the psalms was as natural as breathing, so much so that they tended to despise the Offices and the commentaries used elsewhere:

> The brethren said, 'By what means did the fathers sing the psalms of the Holy Spirit without distraction?' The old man said, 'First of all they accustomed themselves whenever they stood up to sing the service in their cells, to work carefully at collecting their attention and understanding the meaning of the psalms, and they took care never to let a word escape them without knowing its meaning, not as a mere matter of history, like the interpreters, nor after the manner of the translator like Basil or John Chrysostom, but spiritually according to the interpretation of the fathers, that is to say they applied all the psalms to their own lives and works and to their passions and to their inner life and to the war that the devil waged against them.'[30]

The monks said the psalms over and over again, not just at set times; when Bishop Epiphanius, for example, heard of some monks saying the psalms only at the third, sixth and ninth hours, he said, 'the true monk should have prayer and psalmody always in his heart'.[31] The psalms were an authentic way into prayer but they were not for the monks prayer itself; they were a gateway into the life of prayer which is heaven. True prayer, they said, was beyond the repetition of the words of the psalter:

> A monk who has begun to sing the psalms … with understanding and meditation, may refrain from the psalm and sing a song which is beyond the body and which is the song of the angels.[32]

When Abba Macarius went to pray with two young monks, they recited the psalms until he saw the prayer of fire, that is, the Holy Spirit, come down on one of them.[33]

> Abba Lot said to Abba Joseph, 'Abba, as far as I can, I say my little office … what else can I do?' Then the old man stood up and stretched his hands towards heaven. His fingers became like ten lamps of fire and he said to him, 'If you will, you can become all flame'.[34]

It is not the grammatical exegesis of Jerome, the doctrinal interpretations of Augustine, or Cassiodorus' combination of both that is most apparent in Bede's use of the psalms in his writings. While there is always good reason to look seriously at Bede's use of the Bible and to unpack the layers of meaning underlying his choice of quotations, this is especially so when he quotes the psalms. Although he had in his mind the commentaries of his predecessors, the various texts of the psalms, and their liturgical use in church, when he quoted a psalm in his writings—where quotations from the psalms more than any other part of Scripture mingle with the text—it was very often not the Christological meaning nor the moral meaning of a verse that Bede drew out, but its precise application to contemporary life. For Bede the whole Bible was by one author, God, and the psalms were relayed by one author, David, but they were not an end in themselves; through them, God spoke to Christians now, the living word of God clarifying the present and illuminating the one praying. In this he was closer to the monastic hermit tradition of Egypt and it is the Second Conference of Abba Isaac about prayer, as recorded by John Cassian, which best describes Bede's instinctive use of the psalms. In chapter eleven, when Isaac is explaining the heights of prayer, he uses a verse of psalm 103 about prayer and the psalms: 'the high hills are a refuge for the wild goats and so are the stony rocks for the coneys'. The translation of the Hebrew *shaphan*, the hiders, has given scope for many translations: in the Greek Septuagint they are badgers, or rock-badgers, the Syrian versions have hyrax or marmot, while the English identify them as coneys or rabbits.[35] But Cassian, like Cassiodorus, in the Latin tradition has *erinaciis*, hedgehogs: the monk who prays the psalms, he says, becomes a sort of spiritual hedgehog, and is continually protected by the shield of the rock of the Gospel:

> This hedgehog of prayer will then take into himself all the thoughts of the psalms and will begin to sing them in such a way that he will utter them with the deepest emotion of his heart ... as if they were his very own prayer ... and will take them as aimed at himself and will recognise that their words were not only fulfilled by or in the person of the prophet but that they are fulfilled and carried out daily in his own case.[36]

This hedgehog style of prayer was how Bede used the psalms. Two examples must suffice. At the conclusion of his account of the life and death of Cuthbert of Lindisfarne, Bede quotes Herefrith's description of the chanting of psalm 59, 'O God thou has cast us out and scattered us abroad', by the brothers on Farne as part of the ordinary course of the chanting of the psalter at the Night Office. The psalm was a natural part of the sequence of psalms chanted one after the other at vigils for that night, and Bede was well aware of this and of the interpretations of his predecessors. For Cassiodorus, this psalm was a description of how God had shattered the pride of those bound in sins and would recall them into a strong city which was Christ.[37] For Augustine, the casting out and scattering abroad could apply to any temporal suffering endured for Christ, but was especially appropriate to that of the martyrs.[38] But for Bede what was worth recording in detail was how the context of contemporary events was lit up by the phrases of the psalm, illuminating daily experience in Northumbria in his own time.

After Cuthbert's death, there was trouble at Lindisfarne, such trouble that it could be expressed only in these words of despair, 'O God, thou hast cast us out and scattered us abroad'. It is not clear why there was such a falling apart, but this text suggests that many monks had left Lindisfarne. Perhaps with the return of the see of Lindisfarne to Bishop Wilfrid, the monastery was afraid it would not prosper; for a year, until a successor was found for Cuthbert, the monastery was again part of Wilfrid's over-large empire. Perhaps the influence of Iona was pulling the place apart. Perhaps the ambiguous nature of the monastery, in which some monks saw themselves as a community and others as disciples of a holy man, was a cause of their falling apart on the death of Cuthbert who had held them together.[39] Whatever the reasons, the psalm implies that many monks left in distress; it also seems that with the appointment of Eadberht as bishop, a measure of stability returned. 'Turn us again', they seem to have been crying after the death of Cuthbert, and in Bede's lifetime that restoration had happened. The psalm was given an immediate application to human events, rather than a grammatical or Christological meaning. There is a sense of wonder in Bede's account of Herefrith's words, that the psalm should later be seen to have so exactly expressed events and emotions.

Another death also was accompanied by a psalm which Bede saw as significant, that of his abbot Benedict Biscop, which he described in the *History of the Abbots of Wearmouth and Jarrow*. This was psalm 82, of which the second verse was to Bede significant: 'For lo, thine enemies make a murmuring and they that hate thee have lift up their head.' On 12 January, it was being chanted by the brothers in the normal course of the Office in the church at Wearmouth, as the abbot and founder lay dying.[40] Jerome had interpreted this psalm as being about either the church and heretics or the Israelites and their enemies, actual and spiritual; Cassiodorus found in it a doctrinal meaning about Christ and the soul; for Augustine, it was a psalm concerning the church and the world, or Christ and evil. But for Bede, its meaning was deeply personal when related to the death of the abbot who had received him into the community. Well aware of previous interpretations of the psalms, he was yet alert to see a vigorous and lively meaning—not antiquarian, not limited by previous commentary—in relation to present events, and was ready to pray the texts in the light of Christ through his own life and experience. And here his insistence on this interpretation shed a discreet light upon the death of Benedict Biscop; it was, says Bede, a prayer for deliverance and protection in extreme danger at death. The cell of the abbot, dying after great suffering, did not contain a peaceful scene such as the death of Caedmon, Drythelm, Boisil, or Bede himself. For this former thane, a much-travelled, energetic and able man (Bede tells us by his comments on this psalm) death was a bitter agony of soul as well as body. And Benedict Biscop was no less a saint for that prolonged anguish, terror and indignity which all men fear most in dying.

To use the words of the psalms to articulate present terror and grief, as well as joy and wonder, is to discover through the psalms hope beyond hope. As a cry of protest against the inhumanity of man, the words of the psalms are always especially appropriate. Whether the horror is personal or cosmic, whether it is Christ on the Cross, genocide amongst nations, exile from a monastic home, the loss of someone held dear, or the personal anguish of the dying, the words of the psalms express that for which we have no words and at the same time link us into the life of redeeming love: 'Out of the deep have I called unto thee, O Lord, Lord, hear my voice'; 'I am so fast in prison that I cannot get out'; 'O deliver me from them that persecute me for they are too strong for me'; 'My God, my God, why has thou forsaken me?' Bede commended this use of the psalms in these words:

> If any oppressive sorrow has come upon you, either by an injury brought on by others, or by a besetting fault, or by an overwhelming domestic loss, if you grieve for any reason at all, do not murmur against one another or place the blame on God, but rather pray with psalms to the Lord lest the sadness of the world which is death swallow you up; drive the destructive sickness of grief from your heart by the frequent sweetness of the psalms.[41]

It would be possible to make a commentary on the psalter out of Bede's use of the psalms in his writings, and it would be in this mode of interpretative light shed upon the day-to-day personal experience of the one praying. It is this tradition of the use of the psalter as the words through which someone could express his own prayer to Christ, as a means of piercing the heart—compunction—to allow the waters of baptism to flood into the whole person in the present, that Bede inherited, used and lived by.

The psalms were a structure for personal prayer, but Bede did more than use the psalms in this way: he popularised their use by composing a new kind of prayer from them in his abbreviated psalter.[42] It was not a liturgical psalter he had in mind, and this gave him freedom to choose any version of the psalms he liked. He selected the best text he knew, Jerome's third psalter, *iuxta hebraicos.* From this he selected verses from each psalm which could be used as direct prayer or praise, as food for meditation, plea for mercy, protest, contrition, or adoration and exultation. Sometimes one verse alone was used, sometimes several. The verses were also selected so that a sense of the meaning of the psalm as a whole was retained; it would be possible to recall the whole psalm from these clues. There is only one psalm which seems not to have been properly represented, and that is, oddly enough, psalm 136, the great psalm of compunction, *Supra Flumina Babylonis*, 'By the waters of Babylon we sat down and wept'. The verse which is now included as coming from this psalm is, *'beatus homo qui amat dominum'*, a phrase not found in this psalm nor in the psalter, nor indeed in any version of any book of the Bible which I have yet found, nor in any commentary, psalm-collect, or antiphon which I have met. In one of the two early manuscripts which contain the abbreviations, it has been rationalised to *'beatus vir qui timet dominum'* from psalm 111, which is no help at all. It is possible that it is the result of a series of copying mistakes of the verse, *'beatus qui tenebit et adlidet parvulos tuos ad petram'*, 'blessed is he that taketh thy children and throweth them against the stones', but the paleographical errors are unlikely and the choice of sentiment even more so, however carefully glossed.[43] With this inexplicable exception, the text is both a compendium of the whole psalter and a key to each psalm, as well as a collection of phrases admirably suited to private and personal prayer.

The *Abbreviations from the Psalter* was a turning point in the history of prayer, providing a vehicle for popular devotion for the next four centuries. The man who was most enthusiastically vocal in his praise of the psalter as a book for prayer was also an Englishman, also from the north; this was Alcuin, a pupil of the school of Egbert, Bede's colleague, at York. Alcuin recommended the psalter earnestly as the basis of intimate prayer, speaking out of the same tradition as Bede, but carrying it into another mode of self awareness. There is in Alcuin more interior interest in the person praying and his needs, the words of the psalm being seen as the perfect expression of human praise, wonder, love, and delight as well as sorrow, repentance and at times revolt and protest, though with a strong sense also of the external form of the psalms. In this he belongs to the monastic world, and especially to the tradition of the solitary life, and he expanded and elaborated the way indicated by Bede when he wrote:

> In the psalms if you look carefully you will find an intimacy of prayer such as you could never discover by yourself. In the psalms you will find an intimate confession of your sins, and a perfect supplication for divine mercy. In the psalms you will find an intimate thanksgiving for all that befalls you. In the psalms you confess your weakness and misery and thereby call down God's mercy upon you. You will find every virtue in the psalms if you are worthy of God's mercy in deigning to reveal to you their secrets.[44]

For Alcuin, as for Cassian and Bede, the psalms were not an end in themselves, but a preparation for receiving the word of God which is beyond human emotions and needs:

> When the voice of psalmody acts through the intention of the heart, then a way to the heart is prepared for Almighty God, so that He may fill the innermost mind with the mysteries of prophecy or with the grace of compunction, as it is written, 'Whoso offers me praise, he honoureth me; and I will show him the way of salvation of God'. So in the sacrifice of divine praise we are shown the way to Jesus, because when through the psalms the heart is filled with compunction, a way is made by which we come to Jesus. Certainly it is appropriate that when all things are recollected in the mind it cleanses itself and breathes praise of God in the spirit, so that the heavens may be revealed to it.[45]

The psalter was for him also a summary of the revelation and prophecy contained in the rest of Scripture; it was the whole Bible compressed into one text, a *vade-mecum* for the Christian for the whole journey of life:

> In the psalter to the end of your life you have material for reading, scrutinising and teaching; in it you find the prophets, the evangelists, the apostles and all the divine books spiritually and intellectually treated and described; and the first and second coming of the Lord in prophecy.

You will find both the incarnation and the passion; the resurrection and ascension of the Lord, and all the power of the divine words, in the psalms if you peruse them with the intent of the mind, and you will come by the grace of God to the marrow of intellectual understanding.[46]

Alcuin sent a little book to Bishop Arno of Salzburg by the hand of Fredegius, to encourage him in more serious and sustained devotion, and included in it the abbreviated psalter of Bede, thus introducing it with earnest recommendation into the vigorous world of the Carolingians:

For love of you I have arranged to send through my son Fredegius, a little book, containing much about divine matters, that is: short explanations of the seven penitential psalms, also of psalm 119, likewise of the fifteen gradual psalms. There is also in this little book a small psalter which is said to be the psalter of the blessed priest Bede in which he collected sweet verses in praise of God, with prayers from each of the psalms according to the true Hebrew version.[47]

Where Bede had provided, and Alcuin recommended, a selection from the psalms which preserved the shape of the psalm but made it available for personal prayer, a Carolingian writer, copying the form, created a different and even more popular abbreviated psalter. Where Bede had begun from the psalter text, the new compiler began from the needs of the individual for prayers on two themes only. Taking the great themes of compunction, repentance and thanksgiving, he selected only those verses from the psalter that expressed those ideas. Not every psalm, therefore, was represented, and the verses were no longer a key to the full version of the psalm. Moreover, where Bede had used the Hebrew text, he used, he says, a translation better known in his day, which Sigebert of Gembloux later suggested was the Gallican psalter.[48] The changes were deliberate, for the writer, wrongly supposed to have been Einhard, knew Bede's psalter and chose to alter it in these ways:

19

The book of the psalms, although the whole of it is sacred and much better suited than the other books of holy scripture for the celebration of the Divine Office, yet all of it is not convenient for someone who wants to call upon God and beg mercy for his sins. I have therefore taken out those portions which seem appropriate for this purpose, and I have been careful to bring together a little book from them, in which if anything is found to be missing, which is thought to agree with the prayers which have been made, let it be known that what is missing is because it seems to be appropriate not for any of the members of holy church but rather for its head, which is Christ.

Bede the priest of the English made these extracts before me, which would have sufficed for those who want it if it had not been made from that psalter which we call the Hebrew. But because that translation is not used in modern times I did not think it superfluous if I made one from that which at the present time the church sings to Christ over almost all the world.

He who wishes to read this book, must say this three times before he begins, 'O God make speed to save me; O Lord, make haste to help me'. Then he should add 'Glory be to the Father and to the Son and to the Holy Spirit, as it was in the beginning, is now and ever shall be, world without end, amen'. Then he can begin to read, 'Lord, how are they increased that trouble me' etc, to the end.[49]

It is a strange irony that Bede's extracts, which offered a way into the whole psalter, should have been supplanted by an imitator who used the selections for a more subjective purpose. Perhaps changing the text for the one well known through public worship was what determined its popularity. The change to the use of only those phrases which expressed emotion was to be even more far-reaching. Men of a solitary habit of prayer continued to make their own extracts along these lines and increasingly the starting point was not the given words of David, but the personal need and desires of the one praying. The hermit Saint Anschaire (865), for instance, did so:

> from the passages of the Bible which led to compunction he made for himself out of each psalm a little prayer ... he was hardly concerned at all with the order of the words, he sought only compunction of heart.[50]

Whatever the changes in content, the method of abbreviation was introduced by Bede and it remained continually in use. A typical instance of its value is found in the account by Reginald of Durham of another Northern saint, the unlettered hermit Godric of Finchale, a man of much crying and tears. When he first decided to leave his flourishing trade for a life of austerity and prayer, he lived in the wooded country near Carlisle and there someone taught him what Reginald calls 'the psalter of St Jerome'[51]— abbreviations of the psalms which were in fact in the tradition of Bede. Godric, he says, was delighted with it and learned it most carefully by heart. He used this abbreviated psalter for meditation, even when he had learned to read a little by going to school with the children at the church of St Mary in the South Bailly. In his account of this further stage of education, Reginald used words familiar in the tradition of compunction: Godric, he says, learned to listen, read and chant, learning, meditating and ruminating on the psalms. 'Rumination', the metaphor taken from a cow chewing cud, gives a sense of eating the text, absorbing it physically, of so placing it in the memory that it becomes part of the physical person, which is how Bede's psalter was meant to be used. Reginald described Godric sitting on the step of the altar in his oratory at Finchale, holding the psalter *in gremio*, when he saw the Christ Child come out of the mouth of the figure of Christ on the cross and enter into the womb of the Virgin Mary,[52] a startlingly un-theological vision, perhaps, but one which might well have arisen out of prolonged meditation through the psalms on the double *kenosis* of Christ, who 'humbled himself' by taking flesh, as well as by dying on the cross.

The tradition of the abbreviated psalter began with Bede as a memory-device, a reminder of the whole psalm, and also so that by the selected verses the heart could pray and direct itself to God in a way contained within the scriptures. The abbreviated psalter was ideally suited to provide a structure for prayer for less learned but solitary persons, concerned only with the prayer of the heart, and it proved so for other hermits before and after Godric. But it did not remain the possession of the few. A note added to a Durham copy of the abbreviated psalter suggests that it should be used not only by hermits but also by laymen who

> have worldly business, who lie in sickness, who undertake long journeys, sail in ships or go to war; they sing this psalter assiduously and they gain thereby the heavenly kingdom.[53]

The abbreviated psalter contained within it the basis for the prayer of the heart for the Middle Ages, outside as well as inside the monasteries. It had a central place in the articulation of devotion, until a new age found another channel for that same compunction of heart in lengthy meditations which provided other words for the same prayer. This personal and interior prayer was a strong element in a great tradition. When in the eleventh century another man renowned for piety, a monk of Bec called Anselm, was asked to provide such 'flowers from the psalms' for a great and devout lady, he sent her something more. What caught and held the interest of the eleventh century was not Anselm's selection from the psalms, which were quickly dropped, but those majestic prayers and meditations which gave a new form to the prayer of compunction and tears.[54]

At the beginning of his life, Bede learned the psalms in their Christian context; throughout his life the psalms formed him in choir, in his studies and in his cell. At the end of his life it was the psalter which occupied him. He lived the words in which Alcuin expressed his own wondering love of the psalms:

> As angels live in heaven, so live men on earth who rejoice in the praises of God, in the pure heart of psalmody. No mortal man can fully declare the virtue of the psalms. In them are the confession of sins, the tears of the penitent, sorrow of heart. Here is foretold all the dispensations of our redemption, the wondrous delights of heaven's mirth. Here shall you find the Incarnation, Resurrection, and Ascension of the Word of God.[55]

NOTES AND REFERENCES

[1] *Epistola de Obitu Bedae*, in Bede, *Ecclesiastical History of the English People* ed. and trans. B.Colgrave and R.A.B. Mynors, Oxford, 1969, p.581.

[2] For a summary of evidence about Christian customs of prayer in the first centuries, see P. Salmon, *Les Tituli Psalmorum des Manuscrits Latins*, Rome 1959, pp.10-11, and R.Taft, *The Liturgy of the Hours in East and West*, Collegeville, 1986, pp.3-13.

[3] John Chrysostom, Panegyric on the psalter, in *The Holy Psalter*, ed. L. Moore, Madras, 1966, p.xxv.

[4] Cf. L. Brou and A.Wilmart, *The Psalter Collects from V and VI Century Sources*, Henry Bradshaw Society vol.83, London, 1949.

[5] *Epistola de Obitu Bedae*, op cit., p.583.

[6] *Life of Ceolfrith, Abbot of Wearmouth and Jarrow*, trans. D.S.Boutflower, London 1912, cap.4, p.65.

[7] ibid. cap.33, p.81.

[8] Cf. H.M.R.E. Mayr-Harting, *The Venerable Bede, the Rule of St Benedict, and Social Class*, Jarrow Lecture 1976.

[9] *Rule of St Benedict*, cap.18, 'We strongly recommend, if this arrangement of the psalms be displeasing to anyone, that he arrange them otherwise.'

[10] Eddius Stephanus, *Life of Bishop Wilfrid*, ed. and trans. B. Colgrave, Cambridge 1927, cap.LXVII, p.99.

[11] Bede, *Ecclesiastical History*, op. cit., Bk. IV, cap. xviii, p.389.

[12] 'They brought back with them to Britain John (of blessed memory), precentor of the church in Rome, who taught us abundantly the systematic rule of chanting, both by his own living voice and from the musical score.' *Life of Ceolfrith*, op. cit. cap.10, p.62.

[13] Canons of the Synod of Cloveshoe, 747, in *Councils and Ecclesiastical Documents Relating to Great Britain and Ireland*, ed. A.W.Haddan and W.Stubbs, Oxford 1871, vol.111, cap.2, p.366 and cap.27, pp.372-4.

[14] Bede, Homily Bk.2, 25, *In Dedicatione Ecclesiae*, in *Bedae Venerabilis Homiliarum Evangelii*, ed. D.Hurst, Corpus Christianorum Series Latina CXXII, Turnholt 1955, p.368.

[15] ibid. Homily Bk.1, 4, p.30. This is of special interest in determining when the Magnificat began to be sung at evening prayer; the Eastern Churches include it among the odes at Orthos in the morning; the Rule of St Benedict recommends a Gospel canticle at Vespers, but this could be the Nunc Dimittis, as in the Eastern tradition.

[16] *Expositio Bedae Presbyteri in Canticum Abacuc Prophetae*, Corpus Christianorum Series Latina CXIXb, Turnholt 1983, ed. J.E.Hudson, pp.381-409, 'It is the custome … to sing it each week solemnly at the Morning Office' (p.381).

[17] Aethelwulf, *De Abbatibus*, ed. A.Campbell, Oxford 1967, cap. 15, p.40.

[18] Bede, *Ecclesiastical History*, op. cit. Bk.1, cap.xxvi, p.77.

[19] ibid. Bk.III, cap.V, p.227.

[20] Bede, *Ecclesiastical History* Bk.V, cap.24, p.267.

[21] Eddius Stephanus op. cit. cap.2, p.7; cap.3, p.9.

[22] *Biblia Sacra Iuxta Vulgatam Versionem*, Stuttgart 1983, vol.1, for the Jerome psalters *iuxta LXX* and *iuxta hebraicum* compared.

[23] *Life of Ceolfrith* op. cit. cap.37, p.84.

[24] Bede, *Lives of the Abbots*, trans. D.H.Farmer in *The Age of Bede*, Harmondsworth 1965, cap.15, p.201.

[25] *Life of Ceolfrith* op.cit. cap.20, p.69.

[26] cf. R.L.S. Bruce-Mitford, *The Art of the Codex Amiatinus*, Jarrow Lecture 1967, and R.N.V. Bailey, *The Durham Cassiodorus*, Jarrow Lecture 1978.

[27] For discussion of the material in *De Titulis Psalmorum* see B.Fischer, 'Bedae de Titulis psalmorum liber' in *Festschrift Bernhard Bischoff* ed. J.Autenrieth, Stuttgart, 1971, pp.90-100.

[28] Bede, *De Arte Metrica et de Schematibus Tropis*, ed. C.B.Kendall, Corpus Christianorum Series Latina CXXIIA Turnholt 1975, pp.66-171.

[29] ibid. pp142-3.

[30] *The Paradise or Garden of the Holy Fathers* trans. E.A.W.Budge, London, 1907, vol.2, p.306.

[31] *Sayings of the Desert Fathers*, trans. Benedicta Ward, Mowbrays, 1975, Epiphanius 3.

[32] *Paradise of the Fathers op. cit. p.306.*

[33] *Sayings of the Desert Fathers* op. Cit. Macarius, 33.

[34] ibid. Joseph of Panephysis 7.

[35] 'Coney' from 'cuniculus' as in *Fabula de Petro Cuniculo*

[36] John Cassian, 'Second Conference of Abba Isaac' in *Conferences*, trans. E.C.S.Gibson, Nicene and Post Nicene Fathers 2nd Series, reprint Michegan 1973, cap. XI, p.408.

[37] Cassiodorus *Expositio Psalmorum* ed. M.Adriaen Corpus Christianorum Series Latina XCVIII-XCVIIII 1958; 2 vols, vol.1, pp.529-537.

[38] Augustine, *Exposition on the Psalms* trans. A.C. Coxe Nicene and Post-Nicene Fathers, reprint Michegan, 1979, vol.VIII, pp.244-248.

[39] Bede, *Life of St Cuthbert* ed. and trans. B.Colgrave in *Two Lives of St Cuthbert* Cambridge, 1940, cap.xi, pp.285-289.

[40] Bede, *History of the Abbots* op. cit. cap.14, pp.199-200.

[41] Bede, *Commentary on the Seven Catholic Epistles*, trans. D.Hurst, Cistercian Publications, Michegan, 1985, Commentary on James 5:13, pp.60-61.

[42] *Collectio Psalterii Bedae*, ed. J.Fraipont, *Bedae Venerabilis Opera*, Corpus Christianorum Series Latina CXXII, Turnholt 1955, pp.452-470. (See Appendix of this paper for a translation.)
Three ninth century manuscripts contain this text:
a.   Paris, Bibl.Nat.Lat.1153, ff.56v-65v, written in the abbey of S. Denis c.850 (edited A.Duchesne PL C1 cols.569-579).
b.   Paris, Bibl.Nat.Lat.13.388, from St Martin of Tours c.850. (Edited A.Wilmart, *Precum Libelli quattuor Aevi Karolini*, Rome, 1940, pp.143-159. Also E.Martene, PL XCIV cols.515-527.)
c.   Koln, Domkappitel 106, ff.65-71, c.805.

[43] I am indebted to Dom Maurice Bogaert of the Abbey of Maredsous for useful suggestions on this matter.

[44] Alcuin, *De Psalmorum Usu Liber*, Preface, PL.101. col. 465.

[45] ibid. col.465

[46] ibid. 'Ninth Use of the Psalms' col.467.

[47] Alcuin, Letter to Arno, PL.C. col.407.

[48] Sigebert of Gembloux: 'Einhard wrote a life of the Emperor Charles … Imitating Bede who abbreviated the Hebrew psalter, taking out of it all the words that have to do with prayer, he (E) likewise abbreviated the Gallican psalter which we use in Gaul, taking out from it all the verses containing words of prayer.' *Liber de Scriptoribus Ecclesiasticiis*, PL.160 col.566.

[49] *Testimonia Orationis Christianae Antiquioris*, ed. P. Salmon, C. Coeburgh, P. de Puncit, Corpus Christianorum Continuatio Medievalis XLVII, Turnholt 1977, 'Psalterium Abbreviatum Vercellense', ed. P.Salmon, pp.55-78. I am greatly indebted to P.Salmon's excellent discussion and presentation of this text, pp.36-53.

[50] Ibid. p.52, note 2, St Rembert's *Life of St Anschaire* PL118 col.1000.

[51] Reginald of Durham, *Libellus de Vita et Miraculis S.Godrici, Heremitae de Finchale*, ed. Stevenson, Surtees Society, London, 1844, cap.IX, p.42, cap.XVI, pp.58-60.

[52] ibid. cap.XLI, p.99-101.
[53] Ibid. quoted in note 1, p.42.
[54] *Prayers and Meditations of St Anselm of Canterbury*, trans. with introduction Benedicta Ward, Harmondsworth, 1979. See also the penetrating discussion by R.W.Southern in *Anselm of Canterbury: a Portrait in a Landscape*, Cambridge, 1990, pp.91-112.
[55] Alcuin, Epistles IV, 391 PL C col. 497-8

APPENDIX

The Abbreviated Psalter of the Venerable Bede

Translated from the text edited by J. Fraipont, *Collectio Psalterii Bedae*, Corpus Christianorum Series Latina CXXII, Turnholt, 1955, pp.452-470.

The translation is based on Coverdale, Book of Common Prayer, where possible; the psalms and verses are numbered according to Bede's Vulgate psalter with the numbers of the Coverdale version following where they differ.

Ps. 1

1   Blessed is the man that hath not walked in the counsel of the ungodly and hath not sat in the seat of the scornful.

2   But his delight is in the law of the Lord and in his law will he exercise himself day and night.

3   And he shall be like a tree planted by the waterside that will bring forth his fruit in due season.

4   His leaf also shall not wither and look, whatsoever he doeth it shall prosper.

Ps. 2

10   Be wise now therefore, O ye kings, be learned, ye that are the judges of the earth.

11   Serve the Lord in fear and rejoice unto him with reverence.

| 12 | Kiss the Son, lest he be angry and so ye perish from the right way. |

Ps. 3

| 4/3 | But thou, O Lord, art my defender, thou art my glory and the lifter up of my head. |
| 7 | Up, Lord, and help me, O my God. |

Ps. 4

| 2/1b | Have mercy upon me, and hearken unto my prayer. |

Ps. 5

| 2/1 | Ponder my words, O Lord, consider my meditation. |
| 3/2 | O hearken thou unto the voice of my calling, my King and my God, for unto thee will I make my prayer. |

Ps. 6

2/1	O Lord, rebuke me not in thine indignation, neither chasten me in thy displeasure.
3/2	Have mercy upon me for I am weak; O Lord, heal me, for my bones are vexed.
4/3	My soul also is sore troubled; but Lord, how long wilt thou punish me?
5/4	Turn thee, O Lord, and deliver my soul, O save me for thy mercy's sake.

Ps. 7

| 2/1 | O Lord my God, in thee have I put my trust, save me from all them that persecute me and deliver me. |
| 3/2 | Lest he devour my soul like a lion and tear it in pieces, while there is none to help. |

Ps. 8

| 2/1 | O Lord our Governor, how excellent is thy name in all the earth. |

Ps.9

| 1/2 | I will be glad and rejoice in thee, yea, my songs will I make of thy name, O thou most highest.
((Ps.10:13) Arise, O Lord, and lift up thine hand: forget not the poor.) |

Ps. 10/11

| 6/5 | His eyes consider the poor. |

Ps. 11/12

| 3/2 | Help me, O Lord. |

Ps. 12/13

3/2b   How long shall mine enemies triumph over me?
4/3   Consider and hear me, O Lord my God, lighten mine eyes, that I sleep not in death.
5/4   Lest mine enemy say, I have prevailed against him.

Ps. 13/14

7/11   Then shall Jacob rejoice, and Israel shall be right glad.

Ps. 14/15

4   God maketh much of them that fear the Lord.

Ps. 15/16

1   Preserve me, O God, for in thee have I put my trust.
2   O my soul, thou said unto the Lord, thou art my God, my goods are nothing unto thee.

Ps. 16/17

1   Consider my complaint and hearken unto my prayer.
5   O hold thou up my goings in thy paths that my footsteps slip not.
6   Incline thine ear unto me and hearken unto my words.
7   Show thy marvellous loving kindness, thou that art the Saviour of them that put their trust in thee.
8   Keep me as the apple of an eye, hide me under the shadow of thy wings.
16   But as for me I will behold thy presence in righteousness.

Ps. 17/18

2/1   I will love thee, O Lord my strength.

Ps. 18/19

13/12 O cleanse thou me from my secret faults.
14/13 Keep thy servant also from presumptuous sins.
15/14 Let the words of my mouth be always acceptable in thy sight.
16/15 O Lord, my strength and my redeemer.

Ps. 19/20

8/7   But we will remember the name of the Lord our God.

Ps. 20/21

14/13 Be thou exalted, O Lord, in thine own strength, so will we sing and praise thy power.

Ps. 21/22

20/19 Be not thou far from me, O Lord, Thou art my succour, haste thee to help me.

21/20	Deliver my soul from the sword.
22/21	Save me from the lion's mouth.

Ps. 22/23

6	Surely thy loving-kindness and mercy shall follow me all the days of my life.

Ps. 23/24

5	And I shall receive the blessing from the Lord.

Ps. 24/5

1	Unto thee, O Lord, will I lift up my soul.
4/3	Shew me thy ways, O Lord, and teach me thy truth.
5/4	Lead me forth in thy truth and learn me, for thou art the God of my salvation.
7/6	O remember not the sins and offences of my youth, but according to thy mercy think thou upon me.
11/10	For thy name's sake, O Lord, be merciful unto my sin for it is great.
16/15	Turn thee unto me and have mercy upon me.
17/16	O bring thou me out of my troubles.
18/17	Look upon my adversary and misery and forgive me all my sin.
20/19	O keep my soul and deliver me.

Ps. 25/26

8	Lord, I have loved the habitation of thy house.
9	O shut not up my soul with the sinners.
11	O deliver me and be merciful unto me.

Ps. 26/27

1	The Lord is my light and my salvation, whom then shall I fear?
7/8	Hearken unto my voice, O Lord, when I cry unto thee, have mercy upon me and hear me.
9/10	O hide not thou thy face from me, nor cast thy servant away in displeasure.
9/11	Thou hast been my succour, leave me not, neither forsake me, O God of my salvation.
11/13	Teach me thy way, O Lord, and lead me in the right way because of mine enemies.
12/14	Deliver me not over into the will of mine adversaries.
13/15	I believe verily to see the goodness of the Lord in the land of the living.

Ps. 27/28

2	Hear the voice of my humble petitions when I cry unto thee.
3	Do not pluck me away with the ungodly and wicked doers.
7/8	The Lord is my strength and my shield.

Ps. 28/29

2	O worship the Lord with holy worship.

Ps. 29/30

11	Hear, O Lord, and have mercy upon me, Lord, be thou my helper.
13	So that I may sing of thy praise and not be silent, O Lord God, I will give thanks to thee forever.

Ps. 30/31

2/1	In thee, O Lord, have I put my trust, let me never be put to confusion, deliver me in thy righteousness.
3/2	Bow down thine ear to me, make haste to deliver me.
4/4; 6	For thou art my strong rock and house of defence, into thy hands I commend my spirit.
16/17	My time is in thine hand, deliver me from the hand of mine enemies and from them that persecute me.
17/18	Shew thy servant the light of thy countenance, and save me for thy mercy's sake.

Ps. 31/32

1	Blessed is he whose unrighteousness is forgiven and whose sin is covered.
5	I will acknowledge my sin unto thee and mine un-righteousness have I not hid.
7/8	Thou art a place to hide me in, thou shalt preserve me from trouble.

Ps. 32/33

18/17	Behold the eye of the Lord is upon them that fear him and upon them that put their trust in his mercy.

Ps. 33/34

2/1	I will always give thanks unto the Lord, his praise shall ever be in my mouth.
4/3	O praise the Lord with me and let us magnify his name together.
5/4	I sought the Lord and he heard me, yea, he delivered me out of all my fear.

9/8	O taste and see how gracious the Lord is; blessed is the man that trusteth in him.
10/9	O fear the Lord, ye that are his saints, for they that fear him lack nothing.
11b/10b	They who seek the Lord shall want no manner of thing that is good.
21/20	The Lord keepeth all his bones, so that not one of them shall be broken.
23/22	The Lord delivereth the souls of his servants.

Ps. 34/35

1	Plead thou my cause, O Lord, with them that strive with me, and fight thou against them that fight against me.
2	Lay hand upon shield and buckler and stand up to help me.
3b	Say unto my soul, I am thy salvation.
9	And my soul, be joyful in the Lord, it shall rejoice in his salvation.
18	I will give thee thanks in the great congregation.
28	And as for my tongue it shall be talking of thy righteousness and of thy praise all the day long.

Ps. 35/36

6/5	Thy mercy, O Lord, reacheth unto the heavens.
8/7b	How excellent is thy mercy, O God.
10/9	For with thee is the well of life, and in thy light shall we see light.
11/10	O continue forth thy loving kindness unto them that know thee, and thy righteousness unto them that are true of heart.
12/11	O let not the foot of pride come against me, and let not the hand of the ungodly cast me down.

Ps. 36/37

25	I have been young, and now am old, and yet I never saw the righteous forsaken.
28	For the Lord loves the thing that is right, he forsaketh not his that be godly, but they are preserved forever.
40	The Lord shall stand by them.

Ps. 37/38

2/1	Put me not to rebuke, O Lord, in thine anger, neither chasten me in thy heavy displeasure.
16/15	For in thee, O Lord, have I put my trust, thou shalt answer for me, O Lord my God.
22/21	Forsake me not, O Lord my God, be not thou far from me.
22/23	Haste thee to help me, O Lord God of my salvation.

Ps. 38/39

8b   Truly my hope is even in thee.

9   Deliver me from all mine offences, and make me not a rebuke unto the foolish.

11   Take thy plague away from me.

Ps. 39/40

2/1   I waited patiently for the Lord and he inclined unto me and heard my calling.

14/16   Make haste, O Lord, to help me.

17/19   Let those that seek thee be joyful and glad in thee.

18/21   Thou art my helper and redeemer, make no long tarrying, O my God.

Ps. 40/41

5/4   I said, Lord be merciful unto me, heal my soul, for I have sinned against thee.

11/10   But be thou merciful unto me, O Lord.

Ps. 41/42

2/1   Like as the hart desireth the waterbrooks, so longeth my soul after thee, O God.

Ps. 42/43

1   Give sentence with me, O God, and defend my cause against the ungodly people; O deliver me from the deceitful and wicked man.

2   For thou art the God of my strength, why hast thou put me from thee?

Ps. 43/44

26   Arise and help us and deliver us for thy mercy's sake.

Ps. 44/45

           Thy seat, O God, endureth for ever, the sceptre of thy kingdom is a right sceptre,

18b   therefore shall the people give thanks unto thee world without end.

Ps. 45/46

1   God is our hope and strength, a very present help in trouble.

Ps. 46/47

3/2b   He is the great king upon all the earth:

7/6   O sing praises, sing praises unto our God, O sing praises, sing praises unto our King!

Ps. 47/48

15/13   For this God is our God forever and ever, he shall be our guide unto death.

Ps. 48/49

16/15   Truly God hath redeemeth my soul from the place of hell, for he shall receive me.

Ps. 49/50

1   The Lord, even the most mighty God, hath spoken.

8   I will not reprove thee because of thy sacrifices or for thy burnt offerings, because they were not always before me.

9   I will take no bullock out of thine house nor he-goat out of thy folds.

10   For all the beasts of the forest are mine.

11   I know all the fowls upon the mountains and the wild beasts of the field are in my sight.

12   If I be hungry, I will not tell thee, for the whole world is mine and all that is therein.

14   Offer unto God thanksgiving and pay thy vows unto the most highest.

15   And call upon me in the time of trouble, I will set thee free and thou shalt praise me.

23/22   Whoso offereth me thanks and praise, he honoureth me and to him that ordereth his conversation right will I shew the salvation of God.

Ps. 50/51

3/1   Have mercy upon me, O God, after thy great goodness, according to the multitude of thy mercies do away mine offences.

4/2   Wash me thoroughly from my wickedness and cleanse me from my sins.

5/3   For I acknowledge my faults and my sin is ever before me.

6/4   Against thee only have I sinned and done this evil in thy sight.

11/9   Turn thy face from my sins and put out all my misdeeds; make me a clean heart, O God, and renew a right spirit within me.

13/11   Cast me not away from thy presence and take not thy Holy Spirit from me.

14/12   Restore to me the joy of thy salvation and strengthen me with thy free spirit.

16/14	Deliver me from blood-guiltiness, O God, for thou art the God of my salvation and my tongue shall sing of thy righteousness.
17/15	Thou shalt open my lips, O Lord, and my mouth shall shew thy praise.
19/17	The sacrifice of God is a troubled spirit, a broken and contrite heart, O God, shalt thou not despise.

Ps. 51/52

3/2	The goodness of God endureth yet daily.

Ps. 52/53

7/8	Then should Jacob rejoice and Israel should be right glad.

Ps. 53/54

3/1	Save me, O God, for thy name's sake and avenge me in thy strength.
4/2	Hear my prayer, O God, and hearken unto the words of my mouth.

Ps. 54/55

2/1	Hear my prayer, O God, and hide not thyself from my petition;
3/2a	take heed unto me and hear me.

Ps. 55/56

4/3	Though I am sometime afraid, yet put I my trust in Thee.
5/4b	I have put my trust in God and will not fear what flesh can do unto me.

Ps. 56/57

2/1	Be merciful unto me, O God, be merciful unto me, for my soul trusteth in thee; under the shadow of thy wings shall be my refuge until this tyranny be overpast;
3/2	I will call upon the most high God, even unto the God which shall perform the cause which I have in hand.
4/3a	He shall send from heaven and save me.

Ps. 57/58

12/10	Verily there is a God that judgeth the earth.

Ps. 58/59

2/1	Deliver me from mine enemies, O God, defend me from them that rise up against me.
10/9	My strength will I ascribe unto thee for thou art the God of my refuge.
11/10a	God sheweth me his goodness plenteously,

| 17/16b | for thou hast been my defence and refuge in the day of my trouble. |
| 18/17 | Unto thee, O my strength, will I sing, for thou, O God, art my refuge and my merciful God. |

Ps. 59/60

| 13/11 | O be thou our help in trouble, for vain is the help of man. |
| 14/12 | Through God will we do great acts, for it is he that shall tread down our enemies. |

Ps. 60/61

2/1	Hear my crying, O Lord, give ear unto my prayer:
3/4	from the ends of the earth will I call upon thee when my heart is in heaviness. O set me up upon a rock that is higher than I,
4/5	for thou hast been my hope and a strong tower for me against mine enemy.
5/4	I will dwell in thy tabernacle for ever and my trust shall be under the covering of thy wings.
6/5	For thou, Lord, hast heard my desires and hast given an heritage unto those that fear thy name;
8/7	O prepare thy loving mercy and faithfulness.

Ps. 61/62

| 6/5 | In him is my hope, |
| 7/6 | he truly is my strength and my salvation, he is my defence so that I shall not fall. |

Ps. 62/63

2/1	O God, thou art my God, early will I seek thee, my soul thirsteth for thee, my flesh longeth after thee;
3	thus have I looked for thee in holiness, that I might behold thy power and glory;
4	for thy loving-kindness is better than life itself; my lips shall praise thee.
5	As long as I live will I magnify thee and lift up my hands in thy name,
8	because thou hast been my helper, therefore under the shadow of thy wings will I rejoice.

Ps. 63/64

| 2/1 | Hear my voice, O God, in my prayer, preserve my life from fear of the enemy. |

Ps. 64/65

| 6/5 | Hear us, O God of our salvation. |

Ps. 65/66

4/3   All the world shall worship thee, sing of thee and praise thy name.

8/7   O praise our God, ye people, and make the voice of his praise to be heard,

9/8a   who holdeth our soul in life.

20/18   Praised be God, who hath not cast out my prayer nor turned his mercy from me.

Ps. 66/67

2/1   God be merciful unto us and bless us and shew us the light of his countenance.

7/6   God, even our own God, shall give us his blessing.

8   God shall bless us.

Ps. 67/68

2/1   Let God arise and let his enemies be scattered, let them also that hate him flee before him;

4/3   but let the righteous be glad and rejoice before God, let them also be merry and joyful.

Ps. 68/69

17   Hear me, O Lord, for thy loving kindness is comfortable, turn thee unto me according to the multitude of thy mercies,

18   and hide not thy face from thy servant for I am in trouble, O haste thee and hear me.

19   Draw nigh unto my soul and save it, O deliver me, because of mine enemies.

30   Thy help, O God, shall lift me up.

Ps. 69/70

2/1   Haste thee, O God, to deliver me, make haste to help me, O Lord.

5/4a   Let all those that seek thee be joyful and glad in thee.

6/5-6   As for me, I am poor and in misery, haste thee unto me, O God; thou art my helper and redeemer, O Lord, make no long tarrying.

Ps. 70/71

1   In thee, O Lord, have I put my trust, let me never be put to confusion,

2   but rid me and deliver me in thy righteousness, incline thine ear unto me and save me.

4/3-4   Deliver me, O my God, out of the hand of the ungodly, out of the hand of the unrighteous and cruel man,

5/4a	for thou, O Lord God, art the thing that I long for;
10/12	go not far from me, O God. My God, haste thee to help me.

Ps. 71/72

17	Thy name shall endure for ever, thy name shall remain under the sun.

Ps. 72/73

28/27	But it is good for me to hold me fast by God, to put my trust in the Lord God.

Ps. 73/74

12/13	For God is my King of old.
19/20	O deliver not the soul of thy turtle-dove unto the multitude of the enemies, and forget not the congregation of the poor for ever.

Ps. 74/75

10/11	But I will talk of the God of Jacob and praise him for ever.

Ps. 75/76

10/9	When God arose to judgement and to help all the meek upon earth.

Ps. 76/77

2/1	I will cry unto God with my voice, even unto God will I cry with my voice and he shall hearken unto me.
3/2a	In the time of my trouble I sought the Lord.

Ps. 77/78

38	But he was so merciful that he forgave their misdeeds and destroyed them not.

Ps. 78/79

8	O remember not our old sins but have mercy upon us and that soon, for we are come to great misery.
9	Help us, O God our Jesus, for the glory of thy name, O deliver us and be merciful unto our sins for thy name's sake.

Ps. 79/80

3/2b	Stir up thy strength and come and help us.
8/7	Turn us again, thou God of hosts, shew the light of thy countenance and we shall be whole.

Ps. 80/81

2/1	Sing we merrily unto God our strength.

Ps. 81/82

3   Defend the poor and fatherless, see that such as are in need and necessity have right.

4   Deliver the outcast and poor, save them from the hand of the ungodly.

Ps. 82/83

2/1   Hold not thy tongue, O God, keep not still silence,

19/18   and they shall know that thou whose name is our God art only the most highest over all the earth.

Ps. 83/84

9/8   O Lord God of hosts, hear my prayer,

13   O Lord of hosts, blessed is the man that putteth his trust in thee.

Ps. 84/85

5/4   Turn us then, O God our Saviour, and let thine anger cease from us.

6/5   Be not displeased with us forever.

8/7   Shew us thy mercy, O Lord, and grant us thy salvation.

Ps. 85/86

1   Bow down thine ear, O Lord, and hear me, for I am poor and in misery.

3-4   Be merciful unto me, O Lord, for I will call daily upon thee, comfort the soul of thy servant, for unto thee, O Lord, do I lift up my soul.

5   For thou, Lord, art good and gracious, and of great mercy unto all them that call upon thee.

6   Give ear, Lord, unto my prayer and ponder the voice of my humble desires.

7   In the time of my trouble I will call upon thee, for thou hearest me.

11   Teach me thy way, O Lord, and I will walk in thy truth, O knit my heart unto thee that I may fear thy name.

12   I will thank thee, O Lord, with all my heart, and will praise thy name for evermore.

15-16   But thou, O Lord, art full of compassion and mercy, O turn thee then unto me and have mercy upon me, give thy strength unto thy servant and help the son of thy handmaid.

17   Shew some token upon me for good that they who hate me may see it and be ashamed, because thou, Lord, hast holpen me and comforted me.

Ps. 86/87

7   The singers also and the trumpeters shall he rehearse; all my fresh springs shall be in thee.

Ps. 87/88

3/1b   O let my prayer enter into thy presence, incline thine ear unto my calling.

14/13   Unto thee have I cried, O Lord, and early shall my prayer come before thee.

Ps. 88/89

6/5   O Lord, the very heavens shall praise thy works.

15b   Mercy and truth shall go before thy face.

Ps. 89/90

16   Shew thy servants thy work and thy children thy glory,

17   and the glorious majesty of the Lord our God be upon us, prosper thou the work of our hands upon us, O prosper thou our handiwork.

Ps. 90/91

9   For thou, Lord, art my hope.

Ps. 91/92

5/4   For thou, Lord, hast made me glad through thy works.

Ps. 92/93

5   Thy testimonies, O Lord, are very sure.

Ps. 93/94

18   Thy mercy, O Lord, held me up.

Ps. 94/95

6-7   O come, let us worship and fall down, and kneel before the Lord our Maker, for he is the Lord our God.

Ps. 95/96

6   Glory and worship are before him.

Ps. 96/97

10   O ye that love the Lord see that ye hate the thing that is evil, the Lord preserveth the souls of his saints, he shall deliver them from the hand of the ungodly.

Ps. 97/98

3-4   He hath remembered his mercy.

Ps. 98/99

5   O magnify the Lord our God.

Ps. 99/100

2/1b   Serve the Lord with gladness and come before his presence with a song.

3/2   Be ye sure that the Lord, he is God, it is he that hath made us, we are his people.

Ps. 100/101

1   My song shall be of mercy and judgement.

3   I will sing and when thou wilt come unto me I will walk in my house with a perfect heart.

Ps. 101/102

2/1   Hear my prayer, O Lord, and let my crying come unto thee, hide not thy face from me in the time of my trouble.

3/2   O hear me and that right soon.

Ps. 102/103

1   Praise the Lord, O my soul, and all that is within me praise his holy name.

2   Praise the Lord, O my soul, and forget not all his benefits.

3   Who forgiveth all thy sin, and healeth all thine infirmities.

4   Who saveth thy life from destruction and crowneth thee with mercy and loving-kindness.

Ps. 103/104

1   Praise the Lord, O my soul, O Lord my God thou art becoming exceeding glorious, thou art clothed with majesty and honour.

31   The glorious majesty of the Lord shall endure forever, the Lord shall rejoice in all his works.

Ps. 104/105

4   Seek the Lord and his strength, seek his face evermore.

5   Remember the marvellous works that he hath done.

Ps. 106/107

1   O give thanks unto the Lord for he is gracious and his mercy endureth forever.

8   O that men would therefore praise the Lord for his goodness and declare the wonders that he doeth for the children of men.

9   For he satisfieth the empty soul and filleth the hungry soul with goodness.

Ps. 107/108

13/12   O help us against the enemy, for vain is the help of man.

14/13   Through God we shall do great acts and it is he that shall tread down our enemies.

Ps. 108/109

21/20   But deal thou with me, O Lord God, according to thy Name, for sweet is thy mercy; O deliver me, for I am helpless and poor.

26/25   Help me, O Lord my God, O save me according to thy mercy.

Ps. 109/110

2   Be thou ruler even in the midst among thine enemies.

Ps. 110/111

1   I will give thanks unto the Lord with my whole heart.

3   His work is worthy to be praised and had in honour.

7   The works of his hands are verity and judgement.

Ps. 111/112

1   Blessed is the man that feareth the Lord, he hath great delight in his commandments.

7   The righteous shall be had in everlasting remembrance, he will not be afraid of any evil tidings.

Ps. 112/113

2   Blessed be the name of the Lord from this time forth for evermore.

Ps. 113/115

9/1   Not unto us, O Lord, not unto us, but unto thy name give the praise, for thy loving mercy and for thy truth's sake.

Ps. 114/116

4   O Lord, I beseech thee, deliver my soul.

Ps. 115/116

4/12   I will call upon the name of the Lord.

6/13   Right dear in the sight of the Lord is the death of his saints.

Ps. 116/117

2   And the truth of the Lord endureth for ever.

Ps. 117/118

6   The Lord is on my side, I will not fear what man doeth unto me.

7	The Lord taketh my part with them that help me, therefore shall I see my desire upon mine enemies.
9/8	It is better to trust in the Lord than to put any confidence in man.
21	I will thank thee, Lord, for thou hast heard me, and art become my salvation.

Ps. 118/119

7	I will thank thee with an unfeigned heart when I shall have learned the judgements of thy righteousness.
10	O let me not go wrong out of thy commandments.
18	Open thou mine eyes that I may see the wondrous things of thy law.
29	Take from me the way of lying and cause thou me to make much of thy law
36	Incline mine heart unto thy testimonies and not to covetousness.
41	Let thy loving mercy come also unto me, O Lord, even thy salvation according unto thy word.
50	The same is my comfort in my trouble for thy word hath quickened me.
64	The earth, O Lord, is full of thy mercy, O teach me thy statutes.
67	Before I was troubled I went wrong.
68	Thou art good and gracious, O teach me thy statutes.
76	O let thy merciful kindness be my comfort according to thy word unto thy servant.
88	O quicken me after thy loving-kindness and so shall I keep the testimonies of thy mouth.
92	If my delight had not been in thy law, I should have perished in my trouble.
103	O how sweet are thy words unto my throat, yea, sweeter than honey unto my mouth.
108	Let the freewill offerings of my mouth please thee, O Lord, and teach me thy judgements.
116	O stablish me according to thy word that I may live.
117	Hold thou me up and I shall be safe.
124	O deal with thy servant according to thy loving mercy and teach me thy statutes.
132	O look thou upon me and be merciful unto me,
135	and teach me thy statutes.
137	Righteous art thou, O Lord, and true is thy judgement.
149	Hear my voice, O Lord, according unto thy loving-kindness, quicken me, according as thou art wont.

153	O consider mine adversity and deliver me.
159	O quicken me according to thy loving-kindness.
165	Great is the peace that they have who love thy law and they are not offended at it.
169	Let my praise come before thee, O Lord, give me understanding according to thy word.
170	Let my supplication come before thee, deliver me, according to thy word.

Ps. 119/120

2/1	Deliver my soul, O Lord, from lying lips, and from a deceitful tongue.

Ps. 120/121

1	I will lift up mine eyes unto the hills, from whence cometh my help?

Ps. 121/122

6	They shall prosper that love thee.

Ps. 122/123

3	Have mercy upon us, O Lord, have mercy upon us.

Ps. 123/124

8/7	Our help is in the name of the Lord, who hath made heaven and earth.

Ps. 124/125

4	Do well, O Lord, unto those that are good and true of heart.

Ps. 125/126

4/5	Turn our captivity, O Lord, as the rivers in the south.

Ps. 126/127

1/2	Except the Lord keep the city the watchman waketh but in vain.

Ps. 127/128

1	Blessed are they that fear the Lord and walk in his ways.

Ps. 128/129

8.	The Lord prosper you.

Ps. 129/130

1-2	Lord, hear my voice, O let thine ears consider well the voice of my complaint.

Ps. 130/131

1	Lord, I am not high-minded, I have no proud looks.

Ps. 131/132

14/15   This shall be my rest for ever.

Ps. 132/133

3/4   For there the Lord promised his blessing and life for evermore.

Ps. 133/134

1   Ye who stand in the house of the Lord.

Ps. 134/135

3   O praise the Lord, for the Lord is gracious.

Ps. 135/136

26   O give thanks unto the God of heaven, for his mercy endureth for ever.
          ˙[Ps. 136? Blessed is the man who loves the Lord.]

Ps. 137/138

1   I will give thanks unto thee, O Lord, with my whole heart.

8   Thy mercy, O Lord, endureth for ever, despise not then the works of thine own hands.

Ps. 138/139

8/7   If I climb up into heaven thou art there; if I go down into hell thou art there also.

Ps. 139/140

1   Deliver me, O Lord, from the evil man and preserve me from the wicked man.

Ps. 140/141

1   Consider my voice when I cry unto thee.
2   Let my prayer be set forth in thy sight as the incense.
3   Set a watch, O Lord, before my mouth and keep the door of my lips.

Ps. 141/142

8/9   O bring my soul out of prison that I may give thanks unto thy name.

Ps. 142/143

1   Hear my prayer, O Lord, hearken unto me for thy righteousness sake;

˙ For discussion of the verse, see page ?.

2	and enter not into judgement with thy servant for in thy sight shall no man living be justified.
8	O let me hear of thy loving-kindness betimes in the morning, for in thee is my trust; shew thou me the way that I should walk in for I lift up my soul unto thee.
9	Deliver me, O Lord, from mine enemies, for I flee unto thee to hide me;
10	Teach me to do the thing that pleaseth thee, for thou art my God; let thy loving spirit lead me forth into the land of righteousness.
11	Quicken me, O Lord, for thy name's sake and for thy righteousness' sake,
12	for I am thy servant.

Ps. 143/144

1-2	Blessed be the Lord my strength, my hope and my fortress, my castle and deliverer.

Ps. 144/145

2	Every day I will give thanks unto thee and praise thy name forever and ever.
21	My mouth shall speak the praise of the Lord, and let all flesh give thanks unto his holy Name forever and ever.

Ps. 145/146

2/1	Praise the Lord, O my soul, while I live will I praise the Lord, yea, as long as I have any being I will sing praises unto my God.

Ps. 146/147

1	Praise the Lord,
11	for it is a good thing to sing praises unto our God; the Lord's delight is in them that fear him and put their trust in his mercy.

Ps. 146/47

18	He sendeth out his word and melteth them.

Ps. 148

1	O praise the Lord of heaven, praise him in the height.
2	Praise him all ye angels of his, praise him, all his host.
3	Praise him, sun and moon, praise him all ye stars and light.
4	Praise him, all ye heavens, and ye waters that are above the heavens.
11	Praise the Lord, kings of the earth and all peoples, princes and all judges of the world.

12	Young men and maidens, old men and children, praise the name of the Lord,
13/12	for his name only is excellent,
14/13	and his praise above heaven and earth; he shall exalt the horn of his people, all his saints shall praise him.

Ps. 149

1	O sing unto the Lord a new song, let the congregation of saints praise him.
4	He helpeth the meek-hearted.
5	Let the saints be joyful with glory, let them rejoice in their beds.
6	Let the praises of God be in their mouth.

Ps. 150

6	Let everything that hath breath praise the Lord.